Winning Team Building

Practical Guide

A. Luvaren

Copyright © 2024

Practical Guide

1. Introduction

The concept of team building has gained increasing importance in the modern work environment, becoming an essential component for organizational success. Team dynamics are the foundation of a company's performance, influencing productivity, creativity, and employee satisfaction. In a world where business challenges are becoming more complex and global, the ability to create and maintain a cohesive, efficient, and motivated team is a crucial competitive advantage.

The Importance of Team Building

Team building is not just a series of recreational activities or a way to improve employee morale. It is a strategic and intentional process aimed at developing skills, enhancing communication, strengthening interpersonal bonds, and creating a collaborative work environment. Effective teamwork allows for the harnessing of diverse skills and perspectives within the team, leading to more innovative solutions and greater adaptability to market changes.

One of the main benefits of team building is the creation of a strong and positive corporate culture. Well-structured and implemented team-building activities can help develop a sense of belonging and mutual trust among team members. This not only improves job satisfaction but also reduces employee turnover, thereby increasing the stability and cohesion of the group.

Furthermore, team building is essential for improving communication within the team. In many organizations, communication difficulties are one of the main causes of inefficiency and conflict. Through team building, team members learn to communicate more effectively, resolve conflicts constructively, and collaborate towards common goals. This leads to a reduction in misunderstandings and friction, facilitating a smoother and more productive workflow.

Team building is also a key tool for the development of individual team members' skills. Team-building activities often include exercises designed to improve specific skills such as leadership, time management, problem-solving, and creativity. This not only enhances individual capabilities but also strengthens the team as a whole, making it more versatile and capable of tackling diverse challenges.

Objectives of the Book

This book aims to provide a comprehensive and practical guide to team building, exploring not only the fundamental theories and concepts but also the practical applications that can be used in various organizational contexts. The main objectives of the book are:

1. **To provide an in-depth understanding of the concept of team building**: Examining what team building really means, its historical roots, and how it has evolved over time to meet the needs of the modern workplace.

2. **To explore group dynamics**: Analyzing how groups form, develop, and interact, identifying the factors that influence team cohesion, communication, and performance.

3. **To identify different types of teams**: Each team is unique, and this book will explore the various configurations of teams, from functional teams to virtual teams, and how team building can be tailored to each type.

4. **To offer practical tools and strategies for team building**: Providing a range of activities, exercises, and methodologies that can be used by leaders and managers to build and strengthen their teams.

5. **To delve into common team-building challenges**: Exploring the most frequent difficulties that teams encounter, such as resistance to change, interpersonal conflicts, and lack of trust, and offering practical solutions to overcome them.

6. **To promote a holistic approach to team building**: Highlighting the importance of considering team building not just as a series of isolated activities but as an integral part of organizational culture and business strategy.

Structure of the Volume

The book is structured to guide the reader through a complete journey into the world of team building, from fundamental concepts to practical applications. Each chapter is designed to delve into a specific aspect of team building, providing both theoretical foundations and practical tools to implement the strategies discussed.

1. **Fundamentals of Team Building**: This chapter introduces the concept of team building, exploring its definition, history and development, types of teams, and group dynamics. It provides an essential overview to understand the importance and application of team building in the modern context.

2. **Team Building Tools and Techniques**: This chapter focuses on the various activities and methodologies that can be used to build an effective team. It includes practical exercises, role-playing, simulations, and problem-solving techniques, all designed to enhance communication, trust, and collaboration within the team.

3. **The Role of Leadership in Team Building**: Leadership is crucial for the success of team building. This chapter explores how leaders can positively influence team building, providing practical examples and strategies to motivate and inspire the team.

4. **Overcoming Challenges in Team Building**: Not all team-building efforts are successful on the first attempt. This chapter discusses the main challenges that may arise during the team-building process and offers practical solutions to address and overcome them.

5. **Case Studies and Practical Applications**: To provide real-world perspectives, this chapter presents a series of case studies showing how different organizations have successfully implemented team building. These examples offer practical lessons and insights for applying the strategies discussed in previous chapters.

6. **Conclusion and Future Developments in Team Building**: The final chapter summarizes the key points discussed in the book and offers a glimpse into the future developments of team building, exploring emerging trends and new technologies that may influence how teams are built and managed.

Fundamentals of Team Building

What is Team Building?

Team building is a process aimed at improving interpersonal relationships and cooperation within a group of people working together to achieve a common goal. This process includes a series of planned activities that can range from simple icebreaker exercises to complex problem-solving simulations. Team building not only enhances group cohesion but also serves as a tool to develop specific skills such as leadership, time management, communication, and the ability to work under pressure.

In a corporate context, team building is used to strengthen collaboration among team members, improve communication, and increase productivity. It is a fundamental element in creating a positive work environment where employees feel valued, respected, and motivated to contribute to the organization's success.

Team building can take many different forms, depending on the specific objectives you want to achieve. It can include outdoor activities like team games and physical challenges, classroom exercises like workshops and brainstorming sessions, or social activities like corporate dinners and team-building events. Regardless of its form, team building is always oriented toward creating a more cohesive, effective, and motivated team.

History and Development of Team Building

The concept of team building has deep roots in the history of work and human cooperation. Since ancient times, people have understood the importance of working together to achieve common goals. However, team building as we know it today is a relatively recent phenomenon, which began to develop in the 20th century with the rise of modern corporate organizations.

In the 1920s and 1930s, industrial psychologists began studying group dynamics and organizational behavior, trying to understand how to improve worker productivity and satisfaction. One of the most famous studies from this period is the Hawthorne experiment, conducted by Elton Mayo, which demonstrated how social and relational factors within a team could significantly influence work performance.

In the 1960s and 1970s, the concept of team building began to gain popularity as a tool for organizational development. Companies began to recognize the importance of creating cohesive and collaborative teams, and team building became a common practice in training and development programs. During this period, team building focused primarily on recreational and social activities, such as team games and corporate retreats, designed to improve group cohesion and mutual trust.

In the 1980s and 1990s, with the advent of globalization and increased organizational complexity, team building evolved into a more sophisticated discipline, with a greater focus on skills development and problem-solving. Team-building activities began to include simulation exercises, problem-solving workshops, and leadership development programs, all designed to improve team performance and its ability to tackle complex challenges.

In the 21st century, team building has continued to evolve, adapting to changes in the work environment and new technologies. With the rise of remote work and virtual teams, team building has extended beyond the physical boundaries of the office, using digital tools to create cohesion and collaboration among geographically dispersed team members. At the same time, team building has become a central element in creating an inclusive and diverse corporate culture, capable of attracting and retaining talent in a competitive job market.

Types of Teams

In the context of team building, it is essential to recognize that there are different types of teams, each with its own characteristics, challenges, and dynamics. Understanding the differences between these types is crucial for developing effective and targeted team-building strategies.

1. **Functional Teams**: Composed of members working within the same department or functional area of the organization, such as marketing, sales, or human resources. These teams are often characterized by a clear hierarchical structure and specific goals related to their respective business functions.

2. **Cross-functional Teams**: Made up of members from different departments or business functions, these teams are formed to tackle projects or problems that require diverse skills and perspectives. Collaboration among members with different backgrounds is crucial for the success of these teams, and team building can help overcome communication and mutual understanding challenges.

3. **Self-managed Teams**: These teams are characterized by a high degree of autonomy, with members responsible for managing their own work and achieving goals without direct supervision. Team building in this context can focus on developing shared leadership, conflict management, and collective responsibility.

4. **Virtual Teams**: With the rise of remote work, virtual teams have become increasingly common. These teams are composed of members working in different locations, often across different time zones, and primarily

coordinate through digital tools. Team building for virtual teams must address unique challenges such as building trust remotely, managing cultural differences, and creating a sense of belonging.

5. **Temporary Teams**: Formed for a limited period to complete a specific project or solve a particular problem. Once the goal is achieved, the team is disbanded. Team building for these teams often focuses on rapidly building cohesion and managing time effectively.

6. **Project Teams**: Similar to cross-functional teams but with a specific focus on a project. Team members may come from different business functions and work together until the project is

completed. Project teams often require intense collaboration and problem-solving, and team building can help optimize these processes.

7. **Leadership Teams**: Composed of the organization's top managers and executives. These teams are responsible for strategic decision-making and organizational direction. Team building for leadership teams focuses on aligning vision and goals, improving decision-making processes, and fostering collaboration at the highest levels of the organization.

Understanding the type of team you are working with is crucial for developing effective team-building strategies. Each type of team has its own specific needs, and the activities and exercises must be tailored to meet these needs.

Group Dynamics

Group dynamics are the interactions and relationships that develop among members of a team. Understanding group dynamics is essential for effective team building, as these dynamics can significantly influence team performance, communication, and cohesion.

Several factors contribute to group dynamics:

1. **Roles and Responsibilities**: Each team member typically has a specific role and set of responsibilities. Understanding these roles and how they interact with one another is crucial for effective collaboration. Team building can help clarify roles and ensure that everyone understands their contributions to the team's success.

2. **Leadership**: The leader's role in a team is crucial in shaping group dynamics. Leadership style can influence how decisions are made, how conflicts are resolved, and how motivated team members feel. Team building can help develop leadership skills within the team and ensure that the leadership style aligns with the team's needs.

3. **Communication**: Effective

communication is the foundation of positive group dynamics. Team building can help improve communication skills, ensuring that team members can express their ideas, give and receive feedback, and resolve misunderstandings constructively.

4. **Cohesion**: Cohesion refers to the sense of unity and trust within a team. A cohesive team is more likely to collaborate effectively and achieve its goals. Team building plays a crucial role in developing and maintaining team cohesion through activities that build trust and mutual respect among team members.

5. **Conflict Resolution**: Conflict is a natural part of group dynamics but must be managed effectively to prevent it from disrupting the team's progress. Team building can help develop conflict resolution skills, ensuring that conflicts are addressed constructively and lead to positive outcomes.

6. **Decision-Making**: How decisions are made within a team can significantly impact group dynamics. Team building can help improve decision-making processes, ensuring that all team members have a voice and that decisions are made efficiently and effectively.

7. **Motivation**: Motivation is a key factor in group dynamics, influencing how committed team members are to their work and the team's goals. Team building can help boost motivation by creating a positive work environment and ensuring team members feel valued and recognized for their contributions.

By understanding and addressing these factors, team building can significantly enhance group dynamics, leading to improved communication, collaboration, and overall team performance.

2.The Challenges of Teamwork

Teamwork is an essential component for success in any organization. However, working in teams is not always easy and often involves a series of challenges that must be addressed to ensure that the group operates efficiently and harmoniously. In this chapter, we will explore some of the most common challenges that arise in the context of teamwork, including interpersonal conflicts, cultural differences, change management, and stress and burnout within teams. Understanding and addressing these challenges is crucial to improving collaboration and achieving organizational goals.

Interpersonal Conflicts

Interpersonal conflicts represent one of the most common and potentially destructive challenges in teamwork. These conflicts can arise for a variety of reasons, including personality differences, misaligned expectations, different communication styles, and disagreements on how to tackle specific tasks. If not managed properly, conflicts can damage relationships within the team, reduce productivity, and create a toxic work environment.

Causes of Interpersonal Conflicts

1. **Personality Differences**: Each team member brings a unique set of personality traits, values, and attitudes. These differences can lead to misunderstandings and tensions, especially when team members have very different working styles or ways of thinking. For example, a person with a more analytical and methodical approach might clash with a colleague who prefers to make quick, intuitive decisions.

2. **Communication Issues**: Communication is fundamental to the success of teamwork, but it can also be one of the

main sources of conflict. Lack of clarity in communications, the use of inappropriate tones, or misinterpretation of messages can easily lead to misunderstandings and disagreements. Additionally, language or cultural differences can further complicate communication.

3. **Misaligned Expectations**: Team members may have different expectations regarding their roles, group goals, and working methods. If these expectations are not clearly discussed and aligned at the beginning of a project, conflicts may emerge as work progresses. For example, a team member may feel overwhelmed if they believe they have been assigned tasks that are unfairly distributed.

4. **Undefined Roles and Responsibilities**: Lack of clarity about roles and responsibilities can create confusion and conflicts. When team members do not know who is responsible for what, tensions may arise, especially if someone perceives that another member is not

pulling their weight. This uncertainty can also lead to unhealthy competition or a lack of trust.

5. **Conflicts of Interest**: In some cases, interpersonal conflicts may arise from personal interests that conflict with those of the group. For example, a team member may have personal goals that are not aligned with the group's objectives, leading to tensions and disagreements.

Managing Interpersonal Conflicts

Effectively managing interpersonal conflicts requires a proactive and structured approach. Here are some key strategies for addressing conflicts:

1. **Promote Open Communication**: Encouraging open and honest communication is fundamental to preventing and resolving conflicts. Team members should feel free to

express their concerns and opinions without fear of repercussions. Regular meetings and dedicated discussion spaces can help facilitate this communication.

2. **Mediation and Conflict Resolution**: In some cases, it may be helpful to involve a neutral mediator to help resolve conflicts. A mediator can facilitate discussion, help parties understand each other's viewpoints, and work together to find an acceptable solution for everyone.

3. **Clearly Define Roles and Responsibilities**: Ensuring that all team members clearly understand their roles and responsibilities can reduce confusion and prevent conflicts. Setting expectations at the start of a project can help avoid misunderstandings and frustrations.

4. **Provide Conflict Management Training**: Offering team members training on conflict management can help them

develop the skills needed to handle tensions constructively. This training can include negotiation techniques, active listening, and assertive communication.

5. **Create a Positive Work Environment**: Promoting a positive and inclusive work environment can help reduce the likelihood of conflicts. An environment where team members feel respected and valued is less likely to generate tensions and disagreements.

Cultural Differences

In the context of teamwork, cultural differences can represent a significant challenge, especially in an era of globalization and increasing diversity within organizations. Cultural differences can influence various aspects of teamwork, including communication, values, social norms, and leadership styles. If not properly managed, these differences can lead to misunderstandings, tensions, and ultimately, team failure.

Impact of Cultural Differences

1. **Communication**: Cultural differences can affect how people communicate, both verbally and non-verbally. For example, some cultures may prefer a direct and open communication style, while others may adopt a more indirect and reserved approach. These differences can lead to misunderstandings and frustrations if team members are not aware of each other's cultural norms.

2. **Values and Beliefs**: Cultural values influence how people perceive work, success, and interpersonal relationships. For example, in some cultures, teamwork and collaboration are highly valued, while in others, the emphasis may be on individualism and personal initiative. These differences can create tensions if team members do not share the same values or do not understand each other's priorities.

3. **Social and Behavioral Norms**: Social norms, which vary greatly across cultures, can influence behavior within the team. For example, in some cultures, respect for authority and hierarchy is very important, while in others, equality and informality are more appreciated. These differences can cause conflicts if team members are not aware of each other's cultural expectations.

4. **Leadership Styles**: Expectations regarding leadership can vary greatly between cultures. In some cultures, leaders are seen as undisputed authorities who make all decisions, while in others, leaders are expected to be more collaborative and involve the team in decision-making. Differences in leadership styles can lead to misunderstandings and frustrations, especially in international or multicultural teams.

5. **Time and Deadlines**: Different perceptions of time and deadlines can also be a source of conflict. For example, some cultures may have a more relaxed and flexible

approach to time, while others may be very deadline-oriented and punctual. These differences can lead to tensions if not managed sensitively.

Managing Cultural Differences

To effectively manage cultural differences within a team, a conscious and inclusive approach is necessary. Here are some key strategies:

1. **Cultural Awareness**: Cultural sensitivity training can help team members understand and respect each other's cultural differences. This training can include information on different cultural practices, values, and communication styles, helping the team work more harmoniously and collaboratively.

2. **Intercultural Communication**: Promoting effective intercultural

communication is essential to overcoming cultural barriers. Team members should be encouraged to be open and respectful in their interactions, avoiding assumptions and stereotypes. Meetings and discussions should take into account different cultural preferences regarding communication style.

3. **Adaptation of Leadership Styles**: Leaders of multicultural teams must be flexible and adapt to different cultural expectations. This may mean adopting a more collaborative leadership approach in some contexts and a more authoritative one in others, depending on the team's needs. The ability to recognize and respond to cultural differences is a crucial skill for global leaders.

4. **Creating an Inclusive Environment**: An inclusive work environment is essential for managing cultural differences. This means creating a space where all team members feel valued and respected, regardless of their cultural background. Company policies should reflect a commitment to diversity and

inclusion, and leaders should set an example by promoting these values.

5. **Time Management and Deadlines**: To avoid conflicts related to different perceptions of time, it is important to establish clear expectations regarding deadlines and time management from the outset. Team members should discuss and agree on a common approach to deadlines, taking into account cultural differences in time perceptions.

Change Management

Change is a constant in any organization, and the ability to manage change is essential for long-term success. However, change can be a source of stress and uncertainty for team members, especially if not managed effectively. Resistance to change, lack of communication, and fear of the unknown can hinder progress and compromise the effectiveness of the team.

Challenges of Change Management

1. **Resistance to Change**: One of the main obstacles to change management is resistance from team members. People may resist change for various reasons, including fear of losing control, concern about future uncertainty, and attachment to old habits and practices. This resistance can manifest as procrastination, negativity, or open opposition.

2. **Lack of Communication**: Inadequate communication is another factor that can complicate change management. If team members are not informed about the reasons for change, the expected benefits, and how it will be implemented, they may feel confused and anxious. Lack of transparency can fuel rumors and suspicion, increasing resistance to change.

3. **Fear of the Unknown**: Change often brings uncertainty, and fear of the unknown can be paralyzing for team members. This fear can stem from concerns about job security, new responsibilities, or the ability to adapt to

new situations. Anxiety related to uncertainty can reduce the team's motivation and productivity.

4. **Impact on Team Morale**: Significant changes within an organization can negatively impact team morale. If team members perceive change as a threat rather than an opportunity, their engagement and motivation may decrease. This can lead to a drop in productivity and an increase in turnover.

5. **Managing Technological Change**: Introducing new technologies can be particularly challenging to manage. Team members may feel overwhelmed by the need to learn new tools and processes, especially if they do not receive adequate support. Lack of technical skills can increase the sense of insecurity and resistance.

Strategies for Managing Change

To effectively manage change within a team, a structured and inclusive approach is necessary. Here are some key strategies:

1. **Clear and Transparent Communication**: Communication is fundamental to change management. Leaders should provide clear and detailed information about the reasons for change, the goals, and the expected benefits. It is important to address team members' questions and concerns openly and honestly.

2. **Team Involvement**: Involving team members in the change process can help reduce resistance. This can mean asking for their input in planning the change, listening to their ideas and concerns, and ensuring that they feel part of the decision-making process. Active involvement can increase the sense of ownership and commitment to change.

3. **Support and Training**: Providing adequate support and training is crucial for helping team members adapt to change. This can include technical training, coaching, and access to resources that facilitate the transition. Leaders should ensure that team members feel supported and confident in dealing with new situations.

4. **Managing Emotions and Stress**: Change can be emotionally challenging, and it is important to recognize and address the emotional needs of team members. Leaders should be empathetic and supportive, offering emotional support and stress management resources. Creating a positive and reassuring environment can help reduce anxiety related to change.

5. **Celebrating Progress**: Celebrating milestones and successes during the change process can boost team morale and motivate members to continue moving forward. Recognizing achievements and rewarding effort can help create a positive attitude

toward change and foster a sense of accomplishment.

Stress and Burnout in Teams

Stress and burnout are growing concerns in today's fast-paced work environment. High workloads, tight deadlines, and constant demands for performance can lead to chronic stress and, ultimately, burnout. This phenomenon not only affects individual well-being but also compromises the overall effectiveness and cohesion of the team.

Causes of Stress and Burnout

1. **Excessive Workload**: One of the most common causes of stress is an excessive workload. When team members are asked to do too much in too little time, they can feel overwhelmed and unable to meet expectations. Prolonged exposure to high workloads can lead to chronic stress and

eventually burnout.

2. **Lack of Control**: The feeling of having no control over one's work can be a major source of stress. Team members may feel powerless if they believe they have no say in how tasks are assigned, how decisions are made, or how their work is evaluated. Lack of autonomy can reduce motivation and increase stress.

3. **Role Ambiguity**: Uncertainty about roles and responsibilities can cause confusion and stress. When team members do not know what is expected of them or how to achieve their goals, they can feel anxious and frustrated. This ambiguity can also lead to conflicts within the team, further increasing stress levels.

4. **Poor Work-Life Balance**: A lack of balance between work and personal life is another major contributor to stress and burnout. Team members who are unable to

disconnect from work and recharge are at greater risk of burnout. This imbalance can have negative effects on both physical and mental health.

5. **Inadequate Support**: Feeling isolated or unsupported at work can exacerbate stress. Team members who do not receive adequate support from colleagues or leaders may feel alone in facing challenges, which can increase their stress levels. Lack of support can also reduce the team's overall cohesion and effectiveness.

Managing Stress and Burnout

To prevent and address stress and burnout in teams, it is important to adopt a proactive and holistic approach. Here are some key strategies:

1. **Workload Management**: Leaders should monitor workloads and ensure that

tasks are distributed fairly and realistically. If workloads are too high, it may be necessary to reallocate resources, adjust deadlines, or prioritize tasks. Encouraging regular breaks and time off can also help prevent burnout.

2. **Promoting Work-Life Balance**: Encouraging a healthy work-life balance is essential to preventing burnout. Leaders should promote policies and practices that support flexible working hours, remote work options, and time off for rest and recovery. Encouraging team members to disconnect from work outside of working hours can also reduce stress.

3. **Providing Autonomy and Control**: Giving team members greater autonomy and control over their work can reduce stress. This can mean involving them in decision-making, allowing them to manage their own schedules, and providing opportunities for professional growth. Empowering team members to take ownership of their work can increase motivation and job satisfaction.

4. **Offering Support and Resources**: Ensuring that team members have access to the support and resources they need is essential to managing stress. This can include offering mental health resources, such as counseling or employee assistance programs, as well as providing a supportive and collaborative work environment. Leaders should also be available to listen to and address team members' concerns.

5. **Creating a Positive Work Environment**: A positive and inclusive work environment can help reduce stress and prevent burnout. This can involve recognizing and rewarding team members' contributions, promoting open and honest communication, and fostering a sense of belonging and community within the team. A supportive environment can help team members feel valued and motivated.

Summary

Teamwork, while essential to achieving organizational goals, is not without its challenges. Interpersonal conflicts, cultural differences, change management, and stress and burnout are all significant obstacles that teams must navigate. By understanding the causes and implementing strategies to address these challenges, teams can create a more harmonious, productive, and resilient work environment. The ability to effectively manage these challenges is crucial to the long-term success and well-being of both individuals and the team as a whole.

3. Building an Effective Team

Building an effective team is a complex process that requires attention, planning, and a deep understanding of group dynamics. A well-constructed team not only achieves its goals more efficiently but also contributes to the well-being and professional growth of each of its members. In this section, we will explore the various aspects of building an effective team, focusing on four key elements: team member selection, clarity of objectives, role and responsibility definition, and creating a climate of trust within the group.

Team Member Selection

The first stage in building an effective team is selecting its members. Choosing the right people is crucial because it determines the skills, dynamics, and ultimately the success of the team.

Technical Skills and Soft Skills

1. **Technical Skills**: Every team needs members with specific technical skills to carry out the tasks necessary to achieve its goals. These skills vary depending on the sector and type of project but may include analytical abilities, data management, IT competencies, knowledge of specific tools or software, and more. It is important that the technical skills of the team members complement each other, allowing the group to tackle a wide range of challenges.

2. **Soft Skills**: In addition to technical skills, it is essential to consider soft skills, such as effective communication, time management, problem-solving, and emotional intelligence. These skills are crucial for teamwork as they influence how members interact with one another, manage stress, and face difficulties. Soft skills are often more challenging to evaluate than technical ones but can make the difference between a functional and dysfunctional team.

Diversity and Complementarity

1. **Diversity of Background and Perspectives**: Diversity is an added value in any team. Members with different backgrounds, experiences, and perspectives can bring new ideas, stimulate innovation, and improve decision-making. A diverse team is also more resilient, as it can approach challenges from different angles and find more creative solutions.

2. **Complementarity of Skills**: An effective team must not only be diverse but also complementary. Team members should have skills that integrate with one another, allowing the group to tackle all challenges required by the project. Complementarity enables the equitable distribution of tasks and ensures that each member can contribute significantly to the team's success.

Cultural Fit and Shared Values

1. **Cultural Fit**: Cultural fit refers to the alignment of values, norms, and expectations among team members and the organization. A good cultural fit is important because it facilitates collaboration, reduces conflicts, and increases the sense of belonging. However, it is also essential to avoid excessive cultural homogeneity, which could limit creativity and innovation.

2. **Shared Values**: Sharing common values is a crucial factor for the success of a team. Team members must be aligned on fundamental aspects such as integrity, commitment to common goals, mutual respect, and responsibility. Sharing these values creates a solid foundation on which to build trust and collaboration within the team.

Clarity of Objectives

Once the team members are selected, it is essential to establish absolute clarity on the group's objectives. Clear goals act as a compass, guiding the team's actions and keeping members focused and motivated.

Defining Objectives

1. **SMART Goals**: Objectives must be Specific, Measurable, Achievable, Relevant, and Time-bound (SMART). Specific goals prevent ambiguity and provide clear direction. Measurability allows monitoring progress and evaluating success, while achievability ensures that the goals are reachable with the available resources. Relevance ensures that the goals are aligned with the mission of the team and the organization, and time-bounding sets a deadline that stimulates action and a sense of urgency.

2. **Long-term and Short-term Goals**: It is important to distinguish between long-term goals, which represent the overall vision of the team, and short-term goals, which are the concrete steps necessary to achieve the vision.

Long-term goals provide a sense of direction and purpose, while short-term goals help keep the team motivated and focused on the present.

3. **Involving the Team in Goal Setting**: Involving team members in setting goals is crucial to ensuring commitment and motivation. When members participate in goal creation, they feel more responsible and engaged in the process. Additionally, their input can improve the quality of the goals, thanks to their understanding of group dynamics and operational challenges.

Communicating Objectives

1. **Clarity in Communication**: Once objectives are defined, it is essential to communicate them clearly to the entire team. Communication must be transparent and detailed so that all members understand what is expected of them, as well as the timing and methods for achieving the goals. Poor

communication can lead to misunderstandings, frustrations, and inefficiencies.

2. **Using Appropriate Communication Tools**: Communication tools should be chosen based on the team's needs. For example, face-to-face meetings may be useful for discussing long-term goals and addressing complex issues, while digital platforms can be used to monitor daily progress and share real-time updates.

3. **Continuous Feedback**: Communicating objectives should not be a one-way process. It is vital to create feedback channels through which team members can express their concerns, ask questions, and suggest changes. This not only improves understanding of the goals but also strengthens the sense of belonging and collaboration within the team.

Alignment with Business Strategy

1. **Consistency with the Company's Mission and Vision**: The team's objectives must be aligned with the organization's mission and vision. This alignment ensures that the team's work contributes to the overall success of the company and that resources are used effectively.

2. **Integration with Other Business Functions**: The team's objectives must be integrated with those of other business functions. Good integration avoids duplication of efforts, reduces conflicts, and facilitates collaboration between different departments.

3. **Adaptation to Strategic Changes**: The business strategy may change over time, and the team must be ready to adapt. Objectives must be flexible and subject to revision in response to new priorities or opportunities. This requires constant monitoring of the external environment and regular communication with business leadership.

Roles and Responsibilities

After establishing the objectives, it is essential to clearly define roles and responsibilities within the team. Clarity about who does what avoids confusion, overlap, and gaps in work, ensuring that all necessary activities are covered.

Defining Roles

1. **Clear and Defined Roles**: Every team member should have a clear and well-defined role. This includes a detailed description of their responsibilities, main activities, and expected outcomes. Role definition is particularly important in interdisciplinary teams, where skills can vary widely.

2. **Adapting Roles to Skills**: Roles must be assigned based on each member's skills and experiences. This ensures that everyone can operate at their best and contribute

effectively to the team's success.

3. **Flexible Roles**: While it is important to define roles clearly, it is equally essential to maintain some flexibility. In a dynamic work environment, team members may need to take on new responsibilities or adapt to unforeseen changes. Flexibility in roles allows the team to be more agile and responsive to challenges.

Assigning Responsibilities

1. **Clarity of Responsibilities**: Like roles, responsibilities must be clearly defined and communicated. Each team member must know exactly what tasks are entrusted to them and what results are expected. Clarity in responsibilities reduces the risk of conflicts and ensures that all activities are performed efficiently.

2. **Shared Responsibility**: In many cases, responsibilities can be shared among multiple

team members. This approach promotes collaboration and mutual support, as members work together to achieve common goals. However, it is important that shared responsibility is well-coordinated to avoid confusion and inefficiencies.

3. **Accountability**: Beyond defining responsibilities, it is essential to establish a mechanism of accountability. This means that each team member must be responsible for their work and decisions. Accountability promotes commitment and reliability and helps create a work environment where people are motivated to give their best.

Coordination and Collaboration

1. **Coordination Among Team Members**: Good coordination is essential to ensure that all team members work in synergy toward common goals. This requires careful planning, effective communication, and the use of project management tools that facilitate

collaboration.

2. **Cross-Functional Collaboration**: In multidisciplinary teams or those working on complex projects, cross-functional collaboration is crucial. Team members must be able to collaborate with colleagues from other functions or departments, integrating their skills to achieve better results.

3. **Conflict Resolution**: Coordination and collaboration do not always go smoothly. Conflicts may arise due to differences in opinions, skills, or personal goals. It is important to address and resolve conflicts constructively, through dialogue and mediation, to maintain a harmonious and productive work environment.

Building Trust

Trust is the central element on which team cohesion is based. Without trust, team members may be reluctant to share ideas, take risks, or fully commit to their roles. Building a climate of trust takes time, but it is essential for the long-term success of the team.

Interpersonal Trust

1. **Mutual Respect**: Trust is built on mutual respect. Team members must recognize and appreciate each other's skills, experiences, and contributions. Mutual respect creates an environment where people feel valued and safe in sharing their ideas.

2. **Honesty and Transparency**: Trust is also based on honesty and transparency. Team members must be honest in their communications and transparent about their intentions, challenges, and results. A lack of transparency can lead to suspicion, misunderstandings, and divisions within the team.

3. **Mutual Support**: Trust grows when team members support each other, both professionally and personally. This support can manifest in various ways, such as offering help with a difficult task, providing constructive feedback, or being present during times of personal difficulty. Mutual support creates a sense of unity and strengthens the bonds between team members.

Trust in the Leader

1. **Authentic Leadership**: Leaders who demonstrate authenticity can gain the trust of their teams. This means being sincere, acting in line with their values, and showing integrity in all decisions and actions. An authentic leader inspires

 trust and respect, creating a positive influence within the team.

2. **Fairness and Consistency**: A leader

must be fair and consistent in how they treat team members. This includes making unbiased decisions, recognizing contributions equitably, and applying rules and policies uniformly. Fairness and consistency are fundamental for maintaining trust within the team.

3. **Competence and Vision**: Trust in leadership is also based on the leader's competence and vision. Team members must believe that their leader has the necessary skills to guide the team to success and a clear vision of where the group is headed. A competent and visionary leader provides direction and confidence, helping the team face challenges and achieve its goals.

Organizational Trust

1. **Trust in the Organization**: Trust within the team extends to the organization as a whole. Team members must trust that the organization supports their efforts, values their

contributions, and is committed to their professional development. Organizational trust is built through transparent communication, fair policies, and recognition of achievements.

2. **Alignment with Organizational Values**: For trust to develop, the team's values must align with those of the organization. This alignment ensures that members feel part of a broader mission and are motivated to contribute to the company's success.

3. **Consistency in Organizational Practices**: Finally, trust is built when the organization demonstrates consistency in its practices. This means applying policies fairly, upholding commitments, and maintaining open and honest communication with all stakeholders.

Building an effective team is a strategic process that involves careful selection of members, clarity of objectives, well-defined roles and responsibilities, and the creation of a climate of trust. By focusing on these elements, it is possible to create a cohesive and high-performing team that not only achieves its goals but also contributes to the growth and satisfaction of its members.

The journey toward building an effective team is ongoing. It requires continuous attention, adaptation, and development of interpersonal relationships. However, the investment in building a strong team pays off significantly in terms of productivity, innovation, and job satisfaction.

4.Team Building Techniques

Team building is a fundamental process for creating a cohesive and highly efficient workgroup. Team building techniques include a wide range of activities and approaches designed to improve communication, strengthen interpersonal relationships, and develop collaborative skills. These techniques can be applied in various contexts and situations, adapting to the specific needs of the team and the goals to be achieved. In this section, we will explore four main categories of team-building techniques in detail: outdoor activities, ice-breaking and team games, workshops and training, and problem-solving labs.

Outdoor Activities

Outdoor activities are among the most effective and popular team-building techniques, as they combine play with experiential learning. These activities are usually conducted outdoors in natural settings and offer a unique opportunity for team members to interact outside the traditional work environment. Outdoor activities can vary in terms of intensity, duration, and complexity, but they all share the goal of improving group cohesion through shared experiences.

Types of Outdoor Activities

1. **Orienteering**: Orienteering is an activity that requires teams to navigate through unfamiliar terrain using a map and compass. This exercise promotes collaboration, communication, and decision-making under pressure. Team members must work together to find the right path and complete the course in the shortest possible time, which strengthens mutual trust and group cohesion.

2. **Obstacle Courses**: Obstacle courses are designed to test physical endurance,

coordination, and teamwork. These courses can include a series of physical challenges, such as climbing, rope crossings, or trench navigation, which require a high level of collaboration and mutual support. Overcoming these difficulties together helps strengthen bonds among team members and builds a solid foundation of trust.

3. **Treasure Hunts**: Treasure hunts are playful activities that combine puzzle-solving with the search for hidden clues in a specific environment. This activity stimulates creativity, critical thinking, and the ability to work under pressure. Treasure hunts encourage team members to collaborate, share ideas, and coordinate their actions to find the hidden treasure, thus enhancing their ability to work together toward a common goal.

4. **Sports Team Building**: Team sports, such as soccer, volleyball, or basketball, are excellent for developing team spirit and healthy competition. Sports require strategy, communication, and cooperation, all essential

skills in a work team. Participating in team sports events allows members to experience victory and defeat together, which can strengthen the sense of belonging and commitment to the team.

Benefits of Outdoor Activities

1. **Improved Communication**: Outdoor activities often require effective communication to be successfully completed. This helps team members develop and refine their communication skills in a different environment than the workplace, making communication within the team more fluid and natural.

2. **Leadership Development**: Outdoor activities offer numerous opportunities for team members to take on leadership roles, even if temporarily. These roles help identify and develop potential leaders within the group, providing them with the necessary experience to lead in future situations.

3. **Increased Trust**: Facing and overcoming challenges together in an outdoor environment can significantly strengthen trust among team members. Mutual trust is essential for an effective team, as it allows members to work together more harmoniously and productively.

4. **Boosted Motivation and Morale**: Outdoor activities offer an opportunity for team members to relax and have fun together, away from the daily pressures of work. This can positively impact morale and motivation, making the team more energetic and positive when they return to the office.

Ice Breaking and Team Games

Ice-breaking exercises and team games are effective tools to help team members get to know each other better, break the initial ice, and create a more open and collaborative work environment. These games are particularly useful in the early stages of team formation or when new members join an existing group.

Types of Ice Breaking

1. **Creative Presentations**: One of the most common ice-breaking activities is the creative presentation, where team members introduce themselves in an unconventional way, such as through drawings, stories, or personal anecdotes. This type of activity helps break down initial barriers and brings out personal aspects that can facilitate connection among team members.

2. **"Know Your Colleague" Questions**: Another effective method is using "know your colleague" questions, which require team members to answer personal or professional questions about themselves. This type of game not only helps members get to know each other better but can also reveal common interests and skills that can be useful for

teamwork.

3. **Collaborative Challenges**: Collaborative challenges are games that require team members to work together to solve a problem or complete a task. These games can be simple, like building a tower with makeshift materials, or more complex, like designing a strategy to overcome an obstacle. These exercises promote collaboration and creative thinking, stimulating cooperation and integration among team members.

Team Games

1. **Problem-Solving Games**: Problem-solving games are designed to develop critical thinking and collaboration skills. A classic example is the "Marshmallow Challenge," where teams must build the tallest possible structure using spaghetti, tape, and a marshmallow. This type of game encourages team members to think innovatively and work

together to overcome difficulties.

2. **Trust Games**: Trust games, like the "trust fall," where a team member falls backward trusting that their colleagues will catch them, are designed to build and strengthen mutual trust. These games can be powerful tools for developing trust in a team, but they must be managed carefully to ensure all participants feel comfortable.

3. **Communication Games**: Communication games, like "Telephone," where a message must be passed from one team member to another without repeating it, highlight the importance of clear and accurate communication. These games can help improve communication skills within the team and reduce the risk of misunderstandings during daily work.

Benefits of Ice Breaking and Team Games

1. **Facilitating Integration**: Ice-breaking exercises and team games help new members integrate more easily into the team, reducing the time needed to build effective and productive relationships.

2. **Reducing Tensions**: These activities can reduce tensions and anxiety, creating a more relaxed and welcoming environment. A team that feels comfortable together is more likely to communicate openly and collaborate effectively.

3. **Development of Key Skills**: Through these games, team members can develop and refine key skills such as communication, collaboration, problem-solving, and trust. These skills are essential for the success of any team.

4. **Strengthening Team Spirit**: Participating in team games can strengthen the group spirit, promoting a sense of belonging and mutual commitment. This can have a

positive impact on team cohesion and member motivation.

Workshops and Training

Workshops and training are essential tools for the development of individual and collective skills within a team. These sessions can cover a wide range of topics, from communication and leadership to time management and problem-solving. Workshops and training offer team members the opportunity to learn new skills, share knowledge, and work together on specific challenges.

Types of Workshops and Training

1. **Communication Workshops**: Communication is one of the most important skills in a team. Communication workshops are designed to improve the communication skills of team members through practical exercises and simulations. These workshops

can include active listening exercises, feedback techniques, and strategies to improve non-verbal communication.

2. **Leadership Training**: Leadership workshops are designed to develop leadership skills among team members. These workshops can cover a range of topics, such as conflict management, team motivation, and change management. Leadership training is essential to prepare team members to take on leadership roles and contribute significantly to the team's success.

3. **Time Management Workshops**: Time management is crucial for team effectiveness. Time management workshops help team members develop strategies to better manage their time, prioritize tasks, and avoid burnout. These workshops can include planning techniques, the use of time management tools, and strategies to improve personal and group productivity.

4. **Problem-Solving and Decision-Making Training**: The ability to solve problems and make effective decisions is fundamental to the success of a team. These workshops are designed to improve the problem-solving and decision-making skills of team members through practical exercises, case studies, and simulations. These workshops can also teach techniques such as brainstorming, SWOT analysis, and the six-step problem-solving method.

Benefits of Workshops and Training

1. **Skill Development**: Workshops and training provide team members with the opportunity to develop key skills that can improve their individual and collective performance. This can include technical skills as well as soft skills such as communication, leadership, and time management.

2. **Improved Team Cohesion**: Participating in workshops and training

sessions together can strengthen team cohesion, as members share learning experiences and work together to overcome challenges. This can improve collaboration and communication within the team.

3. **Goal Alignment**: Workshops and training can help team members align on common goals and develop a shared vision for the future. This can enhance team motivation and commitment, making them more determined to achieve the group's objectives.

4. **Strengthening Trust**: Participating in workshops and training sessions together can strengthen trust among team members, as they work together to overcome challenges and develop new skills. Trust is fundamental to the success of any team, as it allows members to work together more harmoniously and productively.

Problem-Solving Labs

Problem-solving labs are a highly effective team-building technique for developing problem-solving skills and collaboration within a team. These labs offer team members the opportunity to work together to solve complex problems using a variety of approaches and tools.

Structure of Problem-Solving Labs

1. **Problem Identification**: The first step in a problem-solving lab is to clearly identify the problem the team needs to solve. This could be a real problem the team is facing in their daily work, or a hypothetical problem designed to stimulate critical thinking. Clearly identifying the problem is essential to ensure the team can focus on the most relevant and effective solutions.

2. **Brainstorming**: Once the problem is identified, the team moves on to the brainstorming phase, where as many ideas as possible are generated to solve the problem.

Brainstorming should be conducted in an open and non-judgmental environment, where all ideas are welcomed and considered. This phase allows team members to think creatively and share their perspectives.

3. **Solution Evaluation**: After generating ideas, the team evaluates the possible solutions, considering their feasibility, impact, and potential risks. This phase requires careful analysis and critical thinking to identify the best possible solution. The team must also consider the resources and time available to implement the solution.

4. **Implementation Planning**: Once the best solution is identified, the team moves on to planning the implementation. This involves defining the actions needed to implement the solution, assigning responsibilities, and establishing a timeline. The planning phase is crucial to ensure the solution is implemented effectively and efficiently.

5. **Review and Improvement**: The final phase of the problem-solving lab is the review and improvement of the solution. This involves monitoring the implementation of the solution, evaluating its impact, and making any necessary adjustments. The review and improvement phase is essential to ensure the solution remains effective over time and can be adapted to changing circumstances.

Benefits of Problem-Solving Labs

1. **Development of Problem-Solving Skills**: Problem-solving labs provide team members with the opportunity to develop and refine their problem-solving skills through hands-on practice. This can help the team become more effective in overcoming challenges in their daily work.

2. **Strengthening Collaboration**: Working together to solve complex problems can strengthen collaboration within the team. Team members must rely on each other's

skills and knowledge to find the best solution, which can improve trust and mutual respect.

3. **Encouraging Creative Thinking**: Problem-solving labs encourage creative thinking, as team members are encouraged to generate innovative ideas and explore unconventional solutions. This can stimulate creativity within the team and lead to the discovery of new approaches and strategies.

4. **Enhancing Team Resilience**: Participating in problem-solving labs can help the team become more resilient in the face of challenges and difficulties. The team learns to tackle problems systematically and effectively, which can improve their ability to overcome obstacles and adapt to change.

Team building is a fundamental process for creating a cohesive and highly efficient workgroup. The team-building techniques described in this chapter—outdoor activities, ice-breaking and team games, workshops and training, and problem-solving labs—offer a wide range of options to strengthen collaboration, communication, and trust within the team. By choosing and applying these techniques in a targeted and appropriate way, it is possible to create a strong, cohesive, and motivated team capable of facing any challenge and achieving common goals.

5. Leadership in Team Building

Leadership is a fundamental element in the team-building process. An effective leader can make the difference between a team that operates at mediocre levels and one that excels in achieving its goals. In this context, we will explore leadership styles, the role of the leader in team building, motivation and feedback, leadership skill development, and effective communication within the team. These topics are crucial for understanding how a leader can positively influence team dynamics and guide the team towards success.

Leadership Styles

There are various leadership styles, each with its strengths and weaknesses. The right style depends on several factors, including team composition, business goals, and the specific situation the team faces. The main leadership styles include:

1. **Autocratic Leadership**: In this style, the leader makes all decisions without consulting team members. This approach can be effective in crisis situations where quick and decisive action is needed. However, it may also lead to decreased motivation and commitment among team members who may feel excluded from the decision-making process.

2. **Democratic Leadership**: In contrast, democratic leadership involves team members in the decision-making process. The leader facilitates discussion and encourages participation, but makes the final decision based on group consensus. This style is particularly effective in promoting team cohesion and improving motivation, as members feel they are integral to the decision-making process.

3. **Transformational Leadership**: Transformational leaders inspire and motivate their teams through a clear and engaging vision. They strive to elevate the level of

commitment and creativity within the team, promoting innovation and change. This leadership style is particularly useful in contexts where complex challenges need to be addressed or organizational change is required.

4. **Transactional Leadership**: Transactional leadership relies on a system of rewards and punishments to motivate team members. This style is useful in contexts where tasks are well-defined and goals need to be achieved efficiently. However, it can limit creativity and innovation, as team members may focus only on immediate rewards rather than long-term improvement.

5. **Situational Leadership**: This flexible approach recognizes that there is no universal leadership style suitable for all situations. Situational leaders adapt their style based on the specific needs of the team and the context. For example, they may be more autocratic in crisis situations and more democratic in routine settings.

The Role of the Leader in Team Building

The leader plays a crucial role in the team-building process. They are responsible for creating a positive work environment where team members feel supported and motivated. Here are some key responsibilities of the leader in team building:

1. **Creating a Shared Vision**: An effective leader must develop and communicate a clear and shared vision for the team. This vision serves as a guide, directing efforts toward common goals. The vision should be inspiring and realistic, reflecting both the organization's objectives and the aspirations of the team members.

2. **Facilitating Communication**: The leader must ensure that communication within the team is clear and open. This means promoting an environment where team

members feel free to express their opinions, ask questions, and share information. Effective communication is essential to avoid misunderstandings and resolve conflicts constructively.

3. **Developing Team Skills**: A leader must identify the skills needed to achieve the team's objectives and work to develop those skills among the group members. This may include training, coaching, and mentoring, as well as creating opportunities for team members to develop new abilities.

4. **Motivating the Team**: The leader must be able to motivate the team to perform at their best. This can be done by creating a positive work environment, recognizing achievements, and providing constructive feedback. Motivation is essential to maintain high team morale and ensure that members are engaged and productive.

5. **Conflict Management**: Conflicts are

inevitable in any team, but an effective leader must be able to manage them constructively. This means identifying issues before they escalate, facilitating discussion among the parties involved, and finding solutions that satisfy all team members.

6. **Promoting Diversity and Inclusion**: A leader must promote an inclusive work environment where diverse perspectives and skills are valued. Diversity within a team can lead to innovative ideas and more effective solutions, but only if the leader creates an environment where all team members feel respected and valued.

Motivation and Feedback

Motivation and feedback are two essential elements for keeping a team motivated and productive. The leader plays a fundamental role in both aspects.

1. **Intrinsic and Extrinsic Motivation**: Motivation can be divided into intrinsic and extrinsic. Intrinsic motivation comes from the desire to achieve personal goals, such as professional growth or personal satisfaction. Extrinsic motivation, on the other hand, is driven by external factors such as monetary rewards or recognition. An effective leader must recognize and leverage both types of motivation to keep the team engaged.

2. **Motivation Techniques**: There are various techniques a leader can use to motivate the team. These include public recognition of successes, offering opportunities for professional development, and creating a positive work environment. It is important that the leader adapts the motivation techniques to the specific needs of the team and its members.

3. **The Importance of Feedback**: Feedback is a powerful tool for improving team performance. Constructive feedback helps team members understand their

strengths and areas where they can improve. Feedback should be specific, timely, and future-oriented, so that team members can use it to continuously improve.

4. **Continuous vs. Formal Feedback**: Feedback can be provided continuously or formally. Continuous feedback is informal and given during daily interactions, while formal feedback is structured and usually provided during performance reviews. Both types of feedback are important and should be used complementarily.

Developing Leadership Skills

Developing leadership skills is essential to ensure that leaders are capable of effectively guiding their teams. This development can occur through various methods, including formal training, coaching, and practical experience.

1. **Formal Training**: Formal training includes leadership courses, seminars, and executive development programs. These programs offer leaders the opportunity to acquire new skills and knowledge in a structured environment. Formal training is particularly useful for developing technical and theoretical skills.

2. **Coaching and Mentoring**: Coaching and mentoring are powerful tools for developing leadership skills. Coaching focuses on developing specific leader skills through individual sessions with an experienced coach. Mentoring, on the other hand, involves a long-term relationship with a more experienced leader who provides advice and guidance.

3. **Practical Experience**: Practical experience is one of the most effective ways to develop leadership skills. Facing real situations, managing conflicts, and leading a team through complex projects offer leaders the opportunity to put learned skills into

practice and develop their leadership capacity in a real-world context.

4. **Self-Reflection and Feedback**: An important aspect of leadership development is self-reflection. Leaders must be able to reflect on their actions, identify areas for improvement, and actively seek feedback from colleagues and team members.

Communication Barriers

Communication barriers can hinder effective communication and negatively impact team functioning. Some of the most common barriers include:

1. **Language Barriers**: Linguistic differences can cause misunderstandings and communication difficulties. It is important to be aware of these differences and make an effort to use clear and understandable language.

2. **Cultural Barriers**: Cultural differences can affect how messages are interpreted and communicated. Being sensitive to different cultures and respecting various cultural norms is crucial to avoid misunderstandings. Cultural norms may involve aspects such as tone of voice, facial expressions, and the context in which communications occur. To overcome these barriers, team members must be educated about cultural diversity and promote an inclusive environment.

3. **Psychological Barriers**: Personal biases, anxieties, and concerns can prevent open and honest communication. For example, a team member may be reluctant to express their ideas due to fear of being judged. Leaders must create a safe environment where team members feel comfortable sharing their opinions without fear of negative repercussions.

4. **Physical Barriers**: The lack of adequate communication tools, such as

inadequate technology or unfavorable work environments, can hinder effective communication. Ensuring that team members have access to the necessary tools, such as communication software, appropriate workspaces, and a good internet connection, is essential for facilitating clear and productive communication.

5. **Temporal Barriers**: Differences in time zones and response times can create communication difficulties, especially in geographically distributed teams. To overcome this barrier, it is important to establish clear communication times and use collaboration tools that allow asynchronous communication, such as emails and messaging platforms.

Techniques for Clear Communication

1. **Using Simple and Direct Messages**: To avoid misunderstandings, it is essential to express messages simply and directly.

Avoiding complex jargon and ambiguous phrases helps ensure that the message is easily understandable.

2. **Repeating and Confirming**: Repeating important information and confirming understanding among team members helps reduce the risk of misunderstandings. For example, after a meeting, it is helpful to summarize the agreed decisions and actions.

3. **Adapting the Message to the Audience**: It is important to tailor the message based on the target audience. Considering the audience's level of knowledge, expectations, and needs helps ensure that communication is effective.

4. **Using Visual Aids**: The use of charts, tables, and other visual representations can help clarify complex messages and improve understanding. Visual aids are particularly useful for representing data and processes in a clear and intuitive way.

5. **Promoting Two-Way Communication**: Encouraging two-way communication, where not only the leader communicates but also team members have the opportunity to express their opinions and ask questions, contributes to more effective communication and greater participation.

The Importance of Active Listening

Active listening is an essential component of effective communication and team building. This process involves full engagement in listening to the speaker's message and includes several key aspects:

1. **Paying Full Attention**: Active listening means giving your full attention to the speaker. This involves eliminating distractions, avoiding interruptions, and fully focusing on the message.

2. **Showing Interest and Understanding**: Demonstrating interest through non-verbal cues, such as nodding and maintaining eye contact, helps the speaker feel heard and understood.

3. **Asking Clarifying Questions**: Asking questions to clarify points that are unclear is an important part of active listening. This helps ensure that the listener correctly understands the message.

4. **Summarizing and Reflecting**: Summarizing the key points and reflecting the message back to the speaker helps confirm that the message has been correctly understood and provides an opportunity for clarification.

5. **Being Open and Non-Judgmental**: Active listening requires an open and non-judgmental attitude, which means listening

without forming immediate judgments and being open to the speaker's point of view.

By mastering the techniques of active listening, leaders can greatly enhance their ability to understand their team members' needs, resolve conflicts, and build stronger, more cohesive teams.

This section outlines the crucial role of leadership in team building, emphasizing the importance of leadership styles, effective communication, and motivation in fostering a productive and collaborative team environment.

6.Practical Examples of Team Building

Team building is an essential practice for improving cohesion and productivity within work groups. Sometimes, theory alone is not enough; it is necessary to implement concrete and measurable practices. In this section, we will explore various practical examples of team building that have proven effective in real-world contexts. These examples have been selected to illustrate a range of approaches and strategies that organizations can use to strengthen their teams.

Outdoor Activities

Outdoor activities are a popular form of team building that leverage the natural environment to promote collaboration and problem-solving. Here are some examples:

1. **Treasure Hunts**: Treasure hunts are activities that encourage team members to

work together to solve puzzles and complete tasks. In a well-designed treasure hunt, participants must collaborate to find clues and solve problems, fostering communication and cooperation. For instance, a company might organize a treasure hunt in a local park, where team members must complete challenges related to their work activities. Organizing a trip with all team members can also be beneficial.

2. **Trust Exercises**: Trust exercises, such as the "trust fall," where a participant falls backward and is caught by team members, are designed to build trust among team members. These exercises help overcome psychological barriers and strengthen mutual support.

3. **Shelter Building**: In these activities, teams are tasked with building shelters using limited materials. This challenge requires planning, creativity, and collaboration. Teams must assign tasks, discuss strategies, and work together to create a structure that can withstand environmental conditions.

Ice Breakers and Team Games

Team games and ice breakers are useful for breaking the ice and improving group dynamics. Here are some examples:

1. **Icebreaker Questions and Answers**: During a team building meeting, participants can answer personal and fun questions, such as "What is your favorite book?" or "If you could have a superpower, what would it be?" These games help team members get to know each other better and establish personal connections.

2. **Color Game**: In this game, participants are asked to divide into groups based on the color of an item they are wearing or carrying. Each group discusses and presents a theme related to their chosen color, stimulating creativity and collaboration among members.

3. **Problem-Solving Challenges**: Teams

can tackle complex problems or puzzles that require critical thinking and collaboration. An example is solving riddles or building structures with limited materials. These games not only improve communication but also the ability to work under pressure.

Workshops and Training

Workshops and training sessions can be effective tools for team building, offering opportunities for learning and personal growth. Here are some examples:

1. **Leadership Workshops**: A leadership workshop can help team members develop leadership and management skills. During these workshops, participants can explore various leadership styles, discuss strategies for motivating teams, and practice effective communication techniques.

2. **Conflict Resolution Training**: Conflict

resolution workshops provide team members with the skills needed to address and resolve conflicts constructively. These workshops may include conflict simulations and discussions on mediation techniques.

3. **Innovation Labs**: Innovation labs are designed to stimulate creativity and collaboration among team members. Participants can work on innovative projects, develop new ideas, and test creative solutions to business problems.

Problem-Solving Labs

Problem-solving labs are structured activities that challenge team members to solve complex problems. Here are some examples:

1. **Crisis Management Simulations**: These labs simulate crisis situations where teams must make quick and strategic decisions. Simulations may involve business

emergencies or risk management scenarios, helping team members develop problem-solving and decision-making skills under pressure.

2. **Design Thinking Exercises**: Design thinking labs encourage team members to take a creative, customer-oriented approach to solving complex problems. Through problem definition, idea generation, and prototyping, teams can explore innovative solutions and enhance their ability to collaborate.

3. **Group Projects**: Group projects require team members to work together to achieve a common goal. These projects can include creating a marketing campaign, developing a new product, or designing a technological solution. Group projects help improve collaboration and develop project management skills.

The Role of Technology in Team Building

Technology is playing an increasingly important role in team building, offering new opportunities to enhance collaboration and communication among team members. Let's explore some emerging tools and practices.

Useful Tools and Software

1. **Collaboration Platforms**: Tools like Microsoft Teams, Slack, and Asana facilitate communication and project management. These platforms allow team members to exchange messages, share documents, and track project progress in real time.

2. **Project Management Software**: Tools like Trello and Monday.com help teams plan, organize, and track tasks. These software solutions offer project visualizations, such as Kanban boards and Gantt charts, helping team

members understand project status and deadlines.

3. **Feedback and Evaluation Tools**: Platforms like SurveyMonkey and Google Forms can be used to gather feedback on team building programs. These tools allow for the creation of surveys and questionnaires to assess the effectiveness of activities and identify areas for improvement.

4. **Gamification Tools**: Gamification uses game elements to increase engagement and motivation. Tools like Kahoot! and Quizizz can be used to create interactive quizzes and competitions that stimulate participation and teamwork.

Virtual Team Building

With the rise of remote work, virtual team building has become increasingly relevant. Here are some approaches to promote team building in virtual environments:

1. **Virtual Ice Breaker Activities**: Ice breaker games and activities can be adapted for virtual environments. For example, games like "Two Truths and a Lie" or "Virtual Escape Room" can be played via video conferencing and help break the ice among team members.

2. **Virtual Team Building Meetings**: Virtual team building sessions can include workshops, group discussions, and collaborative activities conducted via video conferencing platforms. These meetings allow team members to interact and work together even when not physically present in the same location.

3. **Online Challenges and Competitions**: Organizing online challenges and competitions, such as cooking contests or gaming tournaments, can be a fun way to engage team members and promote

collaboration. Using screen sharing and chat tools can facilitate interaction and participation.

4. **Virtual Collaboration Platforms**: Tools like Miro and Jamboard offer virtual collaborative workspaces where team members can work together on projects, brainstorm, and share ideas in real time.

The Importance of Networking for Team Work

Building a strong network is crucial for the success of teamwork. Here's why networking is so important:

1. **Resource Sharing**: A well-built network allows team members to access resources and expertise that may not be available within the group. Sharing resources can improve efficiency and foster innovation.

2. **Support and Collaboration**: A network of contacts can offer support and collaboration opportunities. Team members can benefit from advice and support from colleagues, experts, and mentors within their network.

3. **Professional Development**: Building a network allows team members to develop and expand their professional skills. Through interactions and exchanges with industry professionals, team members can gain new knowledge and growth opportunities.

4. **Problem Solving**: Having a network of contacts enables team members to solve problems more quickly. They can consult with experts or colleagues with relevant experience to find effective and innovative solutions.

The Future of Team Building

Team building is continuously evolving, influenced by emerging trends and changes in the world of work. Let's explore some future trends and the challenges and opportunities on the horizon.

Emerging Trends

1. **Increased Focus on Mental Health**: Organizations are beginning to recognize the importance of mental health and well-being in team building. Future activities may include initiatives to support resilience, stress management, and the psychological well-being of team members.

2. **Virtual and Hybrid Team Building**: With the rise of remote and hybrid work, virtual and hybrid team building will become increasingly relevant. Organizations will adopt new technologies and approaches to facilitate connection and collaboration among team members working from different locations.

3. **Personalization and Adaptation**: Future team building activities may be increasingly personalized to meet the specific needs of teams and their members. Using data and feedback to create tailored experiences will contribute to the effectiveness of team building initiatives.

4. **Integration of Technology and Gamification**: Technology and gamification will continue to play a growing role in team building. Future activities may include the use of augmented reality (AR) and virtual reality (VR) to create engaging and interactive experiences.

The Evolution of Team Work

1. **Increased Interdisciplinary Collaboration**: With the growing complexity of projects and business challenges, teams will increasingly consist of members with diverse skills and backgrounds. Interdisciplinary collaboration will be

essential for addressing challenges and finding innovative solutions.

2. **Adaptation to Rapid Changes**: Teams will need to adapt quickly to changes in the market and technology. The ability to work agilely and respond rapidly to new needs will be a key skill for successful teamwork.

3. **Flexibility and Autonomy**: Team members may have greater flexibility and autonomy in their work. Organizations will adopt work models that allow team members to manage their time and activities more independently.

4. **Integration of Sustainability**: Sustainability practices will be increasingly integrated into team building activities. Organizations may adopt initiatives to promote environmental and social sustainability within the team.

Future Challenges and Opportunities

1. **Managing Diversity and Inclusion**: Diversity and inclusion challenges will remain a priority. Organizations will need to address the challenge of creating inclusive work environments and managing group dynamics in diverse contexts.

2. **Work-Life Balance**: Finding a balance between work and personal life will be an increasing challenge. Organizations will need to develop strategies to support team members in managing their work and personal responsibilities.

3. **Innovation and Technological Adaptation**: New technologies and innovations will continue to influence how teams work together. Organizations will need to stay updated on the latest technological trends and adapt quickly to changes.

4. **Development of Future Skills**: The skills required for teamwork will continue to evolve. Organizations will need to invest in training and development to equip team members with the skills needed to address future challenges.

Team building is a crucial aspect of organizational and group success. Through practical examples, such as outdoor activities, team games, workshops, and problem-solving labs, organizations can improve cohesion and collaboration among team members. The integration of technology and virtual team building offers new opportunities to facilitate communication and collaboration in remote environments. Looking ahead, emerging trends and challenges present both opportunities and obstacles for team building, requiring organizations to continuously adapt and innovate to ensure successful teamwork.

7. Tips for Effective Team Building

Team building is a crucial process for enhancing the cohesion and effectiveness of a work group. A well-crafted team building strategy can lead to a more harmonious and productive work environment. Here are 40 detailed tips for executing excellent team building, ranging from planning activities to managing outcomes.

1. **Define Clear Objectives**

Before starting any team building activity, it's crucial to define your objectives. Ask yourself what you want to achieve: improving communication, increasing trust, resolving conflicts, or sparking creativity. Having clear objectives will guide the selection of activities and strategies.

2. **Know Your Team**

To choose the most effective team building activities, it's important to understand your team well. Recognize their preferences, personalities, and existing dynamics. This will help you select activities that meet their needs and expectations.

3. **Involve All Team Members**

Ensure that all team building activities involve every member of the team. Excluding some members can lead to resentment and reduced participation. Every activity should be inclusive and suitable for all.

4. **Choose Relevant and Meaningful Activities**

Team building activities should be relevant to the team's daily work. Activities that reflect work challenges and opportunities can help transfer skills and lessons learned into the work context.

5. **Ensure the Activities Are Fun**

Fun is an essential component of team building. Enjoyable activities not only boost morale but also facilitate learning and cooperation. Make sure the activities are engaging and stimulating.

6. **Create a Safe Environment**

Establishing a safe environment is fundamental for successful team building. Team members should feel comfortable participating actively and sharing their opinions without fear of judgment or retaliation.

7. **Use Ice Breaker Activities**

Ice breaker activities are ideal for breaking the ice and fostering interactions among team members. Examples include mutual acquaintance games or fun activities that stimulate initial communication.

8. **Plan in Advance**

Thorough planning is crucial. Ensure you have all necessary materials and a clear understanding of the timing and logistics. Good planning avoids unforeseen issues and ensures the smooth running of activities.

9. **Adapt Activities to Different Learning Styles**

People learn and interact in various ways. Design activities that cater to different learning styles and preferences, such as hands-on activities, group discussions, or individual exercises.

10. **Set Clear Rules**

Define rules and expectations for the team building activities. This helps avoid misunderstandings and conflicts and ensures everyone knows what is expected during the activities.

11. **Encourage Open Communication**

Open communication is vital for successful team building. Create opportunities for team members to express their opinions and concerns, and encourage constructive dialogue.

12. **Promote Collaboration**

Choose activities that require collaboration and teamwork. Activities that encourage cooperation can help strengthen bonds between team members and improve their ability to work together.

13. **Provide Constructive Feedback**

After team building activities, provide constructive feedback to participants. This helps reflect on what was learned and identify areas for improvement.

14. **Monitor Progress and Results**

Evaluate the effectiveness of team building activities by monitoring progress and results. Use feedback and assessment tools to measure the impact of the activities and make improvements.

15. **Incorporate Activities into Daily Routine**

To ensure that the lessons learned during team building activities have a lasting impact, try to incorporate the concepts and practices into the team's daily work routine.

16. **Promote Diversity and Inclusion**

Team building activities should reflect and promote diversity and inclusion. Ensure that all activities are sensitive to the diverse cultures and backgrounds of team members.

17. **Leverage Modern Technologies**

Utilize advanced team building tools and software to facilitate communication and collaboration. Video conferencing platforms, online collaboration tools, and gamification apps can be very useful.

18. **Organize Outdoor Activities**

Outdoor activities can offer new dynamics and challenges, stimulating teamwork in a different context from the office environment. Consider activities like hiking, team games, and shelter building.

19. **Include Problem-Solving Activities**

Problem-solving activities help develop critical and creative skills. Organize games and simulations that require team members to tackle and resolve complex problems together.

20. **Ensure Activities Are Balanced**

Make sure that team building activities do not favor any team member over others. Activities should be balanced and provide all members with the opportunity to contribute and shine.

21. **Encourage Creativity**

Stimulate creativity through activities that require innovative thinking and original solutions. Brainstorming workshops and creative challenges can help unlock the team's creative potential.

22. **Celebrate Successes**

Recognize and celebrate successes and milestones achieved during team building activities. This can include sharing positive results and awarding members who have made significant contributions.

23. **Align Activities with Business Goals**

Ensure that team building activities align with business goals and organizational strategies. Activities should support and promote the company's vision and mission.

24. **Create a Positive Atmosphere**

Ensure that the atmosphere during team building activities is positive and encouraging. A positive environment fosters participation and engagement from team members.

25. **Be Open to Feedback**

Welcome and consider participants' feedback on team building activities. This will allow you to make improvements and tailor future activities to better meet the team's needs.

26. **Encourage Networking**

Team building activities can be an opportunity to encourage networking among team members. Foster interactions and connections between participants to build stronger relationships.

27. **Choose Activities Suitable for the Group**

Consider the size and composition of the group when selecting team building activities. Activities appropriate for the number of participants and their characteristics will ensure a more engaging and meaningful experience.

28. **Integrate Personal Development Activities**

Incorporate personal development activities that help team members improve their individual skills and capabilities. This may include training sessions on specific skills or personal growth exercises.

29. **Use Experiential Learning

Methods**

Experiential learning activities, such as simulations and role-playing games, can be particularly effective for team building. These methods allow participants to learn through direct experience.

30. **Involve Leaders**

Include leaders and managers in team building activities. The participation of leaders demonstrates the importance of the initiative and can enhance cohesion and communication at all organizational levels.

31. **Create Mixed Work Teams**

Organize activities so that team members work with people they don't frequently collaborate with. This helps break down barriers and fosters better integration between different departments and groups.

32. **Include Reflection Activities**

After team building activities, include time for reflection to discuss experiences and lessons learned. This helps consolidate results and consider how to apply acquired skills to daily work.

33. **Adapt Activities to Changes**

If necessary, adapt team building activities based on changes in the context or team needs. Being flexible and open to adjustments can improve the effectiveness of the activities.

34. **Encourage Reciprocal Support**

Ensure that team building activities promote mutual support and collaboration among team members. Activities that require help and cooperation can strengthen bonds between participants.

35. **Provide Adequate Resources and Tools**

Make sure you have all the necessary resources and tools for team building activities. This includes materials, spaces, and technologies to ensure that activities run smoothly.

36. **Evaluate and Continuously Improve**

After each team building activity, assess the results and seek opportunities for improvement. This ongoing evaluation process helps ensure that future activities are increasingly effective and responsive to the team's needs.

37. **Leverage the Power of Play**

Playful activities can be particularly effective for team building. Games and competitions stimulate engagement and make learning more enjoyable and memorable.

38. **Integrate Corporate Culture**

Ensure that team building activities align with the corporate culture. Activities should reflect the organization's values and practices to ensure consistency and relevance.

39. **Involve External Experts**

Consider involving external experts to facilitate some team building activities. Experts can offer a neutral perspective and new ideas, contributing to a more enriching and professional experience.

40. **Promote Follow-Up**

Follow-up after team building activities is crucial for consolidating results. Organize follow-up sessions to monitor the application of learned skills and discuss further improvements.

Team building is a crucial component for creating and maintaining a cohesive and productive work group. Applying these 40 tips will help you design and implement effective and meaningful team building activities, contributing to improved communication, collaboration, and team morale. With careful planning, a good understanding of your team, and effective management of activities, you can achieve positive and lasting results.

Index

1. Introduction pg.4

2. The Challenges of Teamwork pg.22

3. Building an Effective Team pg.43

4. Team Building Techniques pg.60

5. Leadership in Team Building pg.78

6. Practical Examples of Team Building pg.94

7. Tips for Effective Team Building pg.110

www.ingramcontent.com/pod-product-compliance
Lightning Source LLC
Chambersburg PA
CBHW050307230526
45471CB00005B/2067